Understanding the Electoral College

Catherine McGrew Jaime

Catherine's other books include:

*Understanding the United States
    Constitution*

*The Philadelphia Convention: A
    Play for Many Readers*

*A Conservative Primer on
    Government and Economics*

*Understanding Presidential
    Elections*

Failure in Philadelphia?

*The Philadelphia Convention: In
    Their Own Words*

*Understanding (and Teaching) the
    United States Constitution*

*A Brief Financial History of the
    United States*

Simply Put: A Study in Economics

Creative Learning Connection
8006 Old Madison Pike, Ste 11-A
Madison, AL 35758
www.CreativeLearningConnection.com

What is the Electoral College?

Every four years Americans go to the ballot box and cast their votes for their preference for president, and at least every four years there are complaints and concerns about the process we use to elect our president.

We use something very unique in this country: The Electoral College. The Electoral College is a group of 538 men and women (Electors) from throughout the United States who meet in each state capital and in the nation's capital on one day in December of a presidential election year to formally elect the next president of the United States. Wait, you may say, we vote for president in November of that year. No, not actually. We vote for the Electors who will vote for president.

The next President of the United States will be the man or woman who receives at least 270 electoral votes (a simple majority – half of the 538 plus one), not the one who receives the largest number of popular votes. Generally the same person wins both, but not always. And it doesn't matter, because we don't elect the President of this country by popular votes.

How do we Pick our Electors to the Electoral College?

Each state has the number of Electors equal to the number of Senators and the number of Representatives they have. So currently each state has at least three electors, and as many as fifty-five. (Before 1961, citizens of the nation's capital had no say in our Presidential elections. Then the 23rd Amendment gave the District of Columbia three electors in the Electoral College, the same number as the lowest populated state.)

In forty-nine of the fifty-one "states" (D.C. is treated as a state for this matter), the electors are chosen in a "winner take all" process. In other words, when the votes for those forty-nine states are counted up on and after Election Day, the candidate with the highest number receives all of that state's electors.

The last two states, Maine and Nebraska, do not have a winner take all system. In both states, the candidate with the largest number of votes receives two electoral votes immediately (for the senators' portion). The remainder of the votes are associated with each district (for the representatives' portion).

The winner of each district wins that district's electoral vote. So in theory, multiple candidates can win electors from both of those states. (Sadly, this dilutes the influence of both of those states, rather than increasing it.)

Prior to Election Day, each major political party has selected their slate of electors that will vote in December if their party wins that state.

When the electors meet across the country to cast their ballots, most are not required by law to vote for the candidate of their party (it depends on the laws in their state). But "faithless electors" are rare; seldom will an Elector stray from the vote he/she is expected to cast.

History of
the Electoral College

The process goes back (with some minor tweaking) to the ratification of our Constitution over 200 years ago, and is in the opinion of many (including this author!) one of the most brilliant things our founders accomplished.

Our founders had many options they could have chosen for electing the president. One straightforward way would have been to just have a "popularity contest" and give the office to the man with the most votes nationwide. (They weren't even allowing women to vote at that time, let alone run for office.)

Another way would have been to let the governors of each state cast a vote for the president...Or the House of Representatives could have elected him...And on the options went. They chose none of those. Instead they came up with a system that is not as complicated as it initially appears.

The first thing to remember about this process is that we are not a democracy in this country, we are a **republic**. We have a republican form of government – meaning we vote for representatives, who make decisions for us.

Our founding fathers were very conscious of developing a system that would prevent "mob rule" or the "tyranny of the majority."

Another important point is that **states** were important entities in the eyes of the founders. They were not just forming a **national** government (where we were a large nation operating as one).

They were also forming a **federal** government which brought together the confederation of states. The States were not going to lose their separate identity and function in the process.

The next thing to remember is that our founders tried to set up a form of government that looked out for the interests of both the **small states** and the **large states**.

This was a very real concern during the Constitutional Convention. In fact, it was a concern that almost kept the Constitution from being finished, and from being ratified (accepted by the states) once it was finished.

The founders also had a general mistrust of putting too much power into the hands of everyday citizens. They were very wary of anything that was too "democratic" – believing that it would be too easy for the wants of the majority to trample the needs of the minority in that situation.

All of those concerns led to the system we have come to refer to as the Electoral College.

Federalists and the Electoral College

John Jay

During the ratification process of the Constitution (while the various states debated passing it), Alexander Hamilton, John Jay, and James Madison wrote a number of essays (*Federalist Papers*) to give their thoughts and arguments in favor of the Constitution.

In Federalist Paper #10, James Madison explained the advantages of a republic over a democracy:

"The two great points of difference between a democracy and a republic are: first, the delegation of the government, in the latter, to a small number of citizens elected by the rest; secondly, the greater number of citizens, and greater sphere of country, over which the latter may be extended."

James Madison

James Madison explained more about the **national** versus **federal** idea towards the end of Federalist Paper #39:

"Were it wholly national, the supreme and ultimate authority would reside in the MAJORITY of the people of the Union; and this authority would be competent at all times...to alter or abolish its established government.

Were it wholly federal, on the other hand, the concurrence of each State in the Union would be essential to every alteration that would be binding on all. The mode provided by the plan of the convention is not founded on either of these principles.

In requiring more than a majority, and particularly in computing the proportion by STATES, not by CITIZENS, it departs from the NATIONAL and advances towards the FEDERAL character; in rendering the concurrence of less than the whole number of States sufficient, it loses again the FEDERAL and partakes of the NATIONAL character."

In this particular place Madison is discussing the method they have chosen to make the Constitution amendable, but his arguments also hold true for the way they set up the Electoral College.

Alexander Hamilton

In Federalist Paper #68 Alexander Hamilton defended the Electoral College they were establishing. He used the word "electors," he didn't use the term "Electoral College" which does not come into common usage until later:

> *"And as the electors, chosen in each State, are to assemble and vote in the State in which they are chosen, this detached*

and divided situation will expose them much less to heats and ferments...

They have not made the appointment of the President to depend on any preexisting bodies of men, who might be tampered with before-hand...the choice of persons for the temporary and sole purpose of making the appointment...

Their transient existence and their detached situation, already taken notice of, afford a satisfactory prospect of their continuing so, to the conclusion of it..."

The Advantages
of this System

Some would prefer we go to a popularity contest to elect our President, a more democratic thing to do they claim. If we did that, the power of the larger states would be even greater. All a candidate would need would be to win the most populous states and the contest would be over. Voters in small states would have even less influence than they do now.

And again, we are not a democracy. We are a republic. As the Constitutional Convention came to a close, Benjamin Franklin was asked

"What have you wrought?" His quick response was: "...A Republic, if you can keep it."

Benjamin Franklin

We don't want to get to a place where the majority of the people in our country can trample over the minority just because they are the majority. (Where are the concerns for "minority rights" in this type of discussion?)

In fact, if we go to a popularity contest, a candidate wouldn't even have to have a majority – all they would need would be a plurality (more than anyone else). If at least three candidates are running, that can be far less than fifty percent!

To become president in our current situation, a candidate must convince **enough** voters in **enough** states that he is the man for the job. Even small states have a say with this system.

Additionally, since popular vote is only considered on a state by state basis, the inherent danger of voter fraud is kept to a minimum. If we went to a popular vote, massive voter fraud in just a few places could affect the outcome of the election.

The "Disadvantages" of this System

Someone can be the most popular candidate and still not win the election. This has only happened a handful of times in the more than fifty presidential elections we've held in this country (including 1824, 1876, 1888).

In each of those cases the "popular winner" did not win the Electoral College votes because they were not popular in enough states. In other words, they did not have the wide geographical support necessary.

Can the System be Changed?

Only by a constitutional amendment. This is the most frequently suggested amendment to our constitution – over 500 such amendments have been suggested in the past. Fortunately our founders made it difficult to amend the United States Constitution, and so far no one has succeeded in changing this.

The only other changes that can be made to the system are the way individual states divvy up their electoral votes. (Since the specifics of that is not mandated by the Constitution.)

Colorado tried that in 2004. They were not successful. It was understood by the majority of the voters in Colorado that changing their system would lessen their importance in the Presidential election, not increase it. (With the suggested change, a candidate would have been most likely to win four or five electoral votes from Colorado, rather than zero or nine!)

Columbine

Conclusion

As we get closer to the next Presidential Election, may we think more highly of the Founders who worked so hard to give us an electoral system that has served us well for over 200 years!

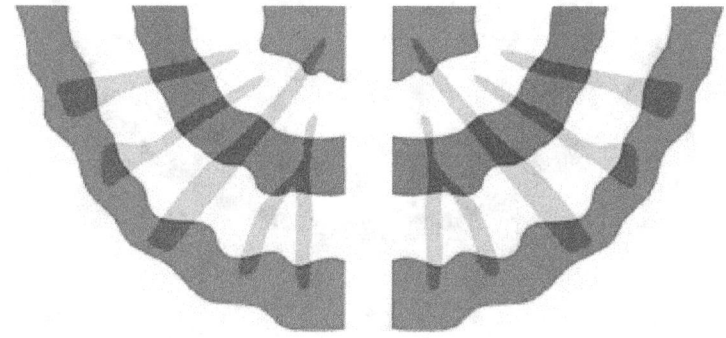

For More Information

There is a great Disney movie (*The One and Only, Original Family Band*) that deals with the electoral votes versus the popular vote from the 1888 election where Grover Cleveland won the popular votes, but Benjamin Harrison won the election with the largest number of electoral votes.

Grover Cleveland
Benjamin Harrison

My favorite line from the movie is when the disappointed grandfather complains, "What's some college got to do with it anyway?"

Aristoplay Game: *Hail to the Chief* : They say it well on their website www.aristoplay.com "Players move around the outside of the board answering questions on presidents and the Constitution, as you become a candidate...Learn how the election process works as well as fascinating historical and geographical facts."

Website Resources

I found the following websites to be useful in my search to understand the Electoral College:

Does my vote count? Teaching the Electoral College by David Walbert: www.learnnc.org/lp/media/lessons/davidwalbert7232004-02/electoralcollege.html

National Archives site with answers to Frequently Asked Questions about the Electoral College:
www.archives.gov/federal-register/electoral-college/faq.html

Great article about the attempt to pass Amendment 36 in Colorado:
www.freecolorado.com/2004/10/36qa.html

Any of the Federalist Papers can be read in their entirety on this website:
http://www.yale.edu/lawweb/avalon/federal/fed.htm

Electoral Votes for the District of Columbia and Each State, Numerical Order
(as of the 2010 census)

State	Votes
District of Columbia	3
Alaska	3
Delaware	3
Montana	3
North Dakota	3
South Dakota	3
Vermont	3
Wyoming	3
Hawaii	4
Idaho	4
Maine	4

New Hampshire	4
Rhode Island	4
Nebraska	5
New Mexico	5
West Virginia	5
Arkansas	6
Iowa	6
Kansas	6
Mississippi	6
Nevada	6
Utah	6
Connecticut	7
Oklahoma	7
Oregon	7
Kentucky	8
Louisiana	8

Alabama	9
Colorado	9
South Carolina	9
Maryland	10
Minnesota	10
Missouri	10
Wisconsin	10
Arizona	11
Indiana	11
Massachusetts	11
Tennessee	11
Washington	12
Virginia	13
New Jersey	14
North Carolina	15
Georgia	16

Michigan	16
Ohio	18
Illinois	20
Pennsylvania	20
Florida	29
New York	29
Texas	38
California	55
Total	**538**

Electoral Votes
Alphabetically
(as of the 2010 census)

State	Votes
Alabama	9
Alaska	3
Arizona	11
Arkansas	6
California	55
Colorado	9
Connecticut	7
Delaware	3
District of Columbia	3
Florida	29
Georgia	16
Hawaii	4

Idaho	4
Illinois	20
Indiana	11
Iowa	6
Kansas	6
Kentucky	8
Louisiana	8
Maine	4
Maryland	10
Massachusetts	11
Michigan	16
Minnesota	10
Mississippi	6
Missouri	10
Montana	3
Nebraska	5

Nevada	6
New Hampshire	4
New Jersey	14
New Mexico	5
New York	29
North Carolina	15
North Dakota	3
Ohio	18
Oklahoma	7
Oregon	7
Pennsylvania	20
Rhode Island	4
South Carolina	9
South Dakota	3
Tennessee	11
Texas	38

Utah	6
Vermont	3
Virginia	13
Washington	12
West Virginia	5
Wisconsin	10
Wyoming	3
Total	**538**

About the Author

Catherine Jaime is the co-author of an article on the Electoral College in a national publication on the American Government. She has also authored several books dealing with government and economics.

Catherine firmly believes in the importance of the U.S. Constitution and the free market, and it shows in her writings.

Catherine has been teaching high school economics and

government for almost twenty years. She loves sharing her passion for these subjects with her students and her readers.

Catherine did her under-graduate work at the Sloan School of Management at the Massachusetts Institute of Technology, in Cambridge, Massachusetts, and has continued her economics training through the Foundation for Teaching Economics and the Foundation for Economic Education.

Catherine can be reached at cmmjaime@alum.mit.edu,

and more of her books (on this topic and many others!) can be found on her website, www.CatherineJaime.com, as well as on many major book retailer sites.

As an indie author, Catherine would be thrilled if you would do her the honor of a review upon completion of her book.

www.ingramcontent.com/pod-product-compliance
Lightning Source LLC
Chambersburg PA
CBHW071303280526
45788CB00004B/1821